ESSENTIAL
ENGLISH
GRAMMAR

Raju Suppiah

PARTRIDGE

ISBN: Hardcover   978-1-4828-9586-5
            Softcover   978-1-4828-9585-8
            eBook   978-1-4828-9260-4

Print information available on the last page.

To order additional copies of this book, contact
Toll Free 800 101 2657 (Singapore)
Toll Free 1 800 81 7340 (Malaysia)
orders.singapore@partridgepublishing.com

www.partridgepublishing.com/singapore

PREFACE

Essential English Grammar is written for all learners of the English language. Non-native English learners often use the vernacular to translate directly from their own language, leading to unsuitable situations in expressing effectively in English. This is partly due to a lack of understanding of English grammar speech and relevant parts of the language structure.

Care has been taken to state rules and definitions of grammar in simple language to help students gain a better understanding of the subject.

The material can help both students and teachers of SPM, SPMV, MCE, MUET, Cambridge "O" and "A" level Examinations like TOFEL, TOSEL, IELTS and other relevant examinations. Teachers teaching English grammar should find this book useful.

I hope this book will help users achieve a better standard in reading, writing and in communicating effectively in English.

Raju Suppiah FRC AMN

Special thanks to Partridge Publishing who helped me in completing this book.

Jen Robins, my Publishing Consultant

Timothy Brendon, my Marketing Consultant

Rey Santos, my Publishing Service Associate

Chris Lodovice, from the Author Learning Center

Carlo Tuvilla, my Cover Designer

Jimmy Achapero Jr., my Interior Designer

CONTENTS

CHAPTER 1
NOUNS

Types of Nouns
Proper Nouns
Common Nouns
Countable and Uncountable Nouns
Gender in Nouns
Abstract Nouns
Collective Nouns
Compound Nouns
Numbers - Singular and Plural
Exercises

NOUNS

A **NOUN** is a word used as a person, place, thing or an abstract idea.

The different types of nouns are:

1. Common Nouns
2. Proper Nouns
3. Count or Non Count Nouns also called Countable and Uncountable Nouns
4. Singular and Plural Nouns (Numbers)
5. Masculine and Feminine Nouns (Gender)
6. Abstract Nouns
7. Collective Nouns
8. Compound Nouns

COMMON NOUNS

Common Nouns are names of things commonly found.

E.g. book, pen, dog, pencil.

They can be concrete nouns which are things which we can see, hear, smell, taste or feel.

They can be either Singular or Plural in number.

Eg.	Singular	Plural
	book	books
	box	boxes
	church	churches

watch	watches
hero	heroes
potato	potatoes
knife	knives
life	lives
wife	wives
lady	ladies
foot	feet
goose	geese
piano	pianos
solo	solos
valley	valleys
mouse	mice
child	children
man	men
woman	women
syllabus	syllabi or syllabuses

PROPER NOUNS

These are either names of people or names of places.

Eg. John Smith   Ali Nordin   Rajendran   Ipoh   Paris
Malaysia

Names of days of the week and names of months of the year are also Proper Nouns. These are always written with Capital Letters.

Common Nouns	Proper Nouns
Plants (Trees)	Ash, Chestnut
Vegetables	Cabbage, Spinach

Flower	Rose, Hibiscus
Fruit	Apples, Bananas
Country	China

COUNTABLE AND UNCOUNTABLE NOUNS

These are also known as Count and Noncount Nouns They are usually used with words such as *some, any, more, a little and much.*

Air, water, sugar, acre, kilogram are uncountable nouns

Eg. The baby wants some milk,
The lady bought a kilogram of sugar.
They poured some water over the plants.

GENDER IN NOUNS

The four Genders are Masculine, Feminine, Common and Neuter Genders:

The masculine gender refers to things that are male.

Eg. King, brother, lion, uncle, grandfather, dog, drake.

The feminine gender refers to things that are female.

Eg. Queen, sister, lioness, auntie, grandmother, bitch. duck.

The Common Gender. Common to either sex.

Eg. baby, student, child salesperson.

The neuter gender. This refers to inanimate objects without sex.

Eg. tree. pen, television, restaurant.

ABSTRACT NOUNS

Things that we cannot touch but feel are Abstract Nouns. Examples of Abstract Nouns are:

Love, honesty, beauty, truth, anger, danger, hatred and jealousy.

Eg. Love is blind but the neighbours are not.
Honesty is the best policy.
Truth always prevails.
Rahaman showed his anger instantly.
There is danger when there is a fire.
She showed that she was angry.
Her jealousy made her do what she did.

COLLECTIVE NOUNS

Collective Nouns refer to a number or group of people, animals or things of the same kind.

Eg. an army of soldiers   a litter of cubs
    a board of directors   a school of whales
    a choir of singers   a shoal of herring
    a gang of labourers   a swarm of insects
    a gang of thieves   a swarm of bees
    a herd of buffaloes   a tribe of natives
    a herd of cattle   a troop of monkeys
    A flight of aeroplanes   a troupe of dancers
    a staff of teachers   a band of musicians

COMPOUND NOUNS

A compound noun is made up of two nouns.

Eg.	after and noon	-	afternoon
	well and known	-	well-known
	bed and room	-	bedroom
	under and ground	-	underground
	cow and boy	-	cowboy
	wash and room	-	washroom
	ear and ring	-	earring
	wrist and watch	-	wristwatch

Eg. We placed the cupboard in the bedroom.
    The cowboy managed to find the stray cattle.
    They hid the treasure underground.
    The student bought a new wristwatch.

NOUNS - NUMBERS

A SINGULAR noun denotes one person or one thing while a PLURAL noun denotes more than one person or thing.

1. A plural noun is formed by adding an 's' to the singular noun.

   Eg. book   -   books
        pen   -   pens
        boy   -   boys
        girl   -   girls

2. When rhe noun ends with 'x', 'ss' or 'ch' we add 'es' to make the singular into plural.

   Eg. box   -   boxes
        church -   churches
        glass   -   glasses
        watch   -   watches

3. Most nouns ending with an 'o' also take an 'es' into the plural.

   Eg. potato - potatoes   exceptions:
        cargo   - cargoes   piano   -   pianos
        buffalo - buffaloes bamboo -   bamboos
        mango   - mangoes   solo   -   solos

4. Nouns ending with 'f' or 'fe' form their plural by changing the 'f' or 'fe' into 'v' and adding 'es'.

Eg.	calf	-	calve	exceptions:		
	leaf	-	leaves	chief	-	chiefs
	knife	-	knives	roof	-	roofs
	life	-	lives	gulf	-	gulfs

5. Nouns ending with 'y' form their plural by changing the 'y' into 'i' and adding 'es'.

Eg.	baby	-	babies	exceptions:		
	lady	-	ladies	valley	-	valleys
	fly	-	flies	day	-	days
	story	-	stories	kidney	-	kidneys

6. Some nouns (not all) having a double 'oo' written in plural change the 'oo' to 'ee'.

Eg.	foot	-	feet
	goose	-	geese

7. Several nouns have a different word form in the plural.

Eg.	man	-	men
	woman	-	women
	child	-	children
	mouse	-	mice

8. Some nouns have the singular and plural alike.

Eg.	sheep	-	sheep
	deer	-	deer
	fish	-	fish
	cod	-	cod
	trout	-	trout

salmon	-	salmon
herring	-	herring
poultry	-	poultry
cattle	-	cattle

9. Some nouns are used only in the plural

    Eg.   spectacles, trousers, measles, draughts, mathematics and news.

10. Unusual words.

    Eg.   radius - radii
           person - people
           syllabus - syllabi or syllabuses

Some examples of Singular and plural nouns:

SINGULAR	PLURAL
cat	cats
bat	bats
rat	rats
book	books
pen	pens
box	boxes
fox	foxes
brush	brushes
glass	glasses
watch	watches
army	armies
lady	ladies
baby	babies

valley	valleys
leaf	leaves
shelf	shelves
wolf	wolves
thief	thieves
wife	wives
hero	heroes
potato	potatoes
piano	pianos
bamboo	bamboos
mosquito	mosquitoes
mango	mangoes
mouse	mice
sheep	sheep
fish	fish
child	children
foot	feet
goose	geese
man	men
woman	women
deer	deer
dozen	dozen
brother-in-law	brothers-in-law
by-law	by-laws
passer-by	passers-by
son-in-law	sons-in-law
radius	radii
medium	media
memorandum	memoranda
syllabus	syllabi or syllabuses

Exercise: Underline the nouns in the following sentences and identify the type of noun. [Answers in page 133]

1. The boy walked for several hours.

2. Kuala Lumpur is a very busy city in Malaysia.

3. They went to the sea and caught a shoal of herring.

4. Honesty is the best policy.

5. This afternoon we will watch a game of soccer.

6. The members of the staff had a meeting this morning.

7. The sultan waited for his subjects to arrive.

8. Place this hammer under the table.

9. John Smith went to school very early in the morning.

10. The Professor was an honour to his profession.

CHAPTER 2
VERBS AND TENSES

Types of verbs Regular and Irregular verbs
Stative verbs
Tenses- Simple Present. Past Tense and
Future Tense. Present Perfect and Present
Perfect Continuous Tenses. Past Perfect
and Past perfect Continuous Tenses.
The Future Tenses.
Exercises.

ENGLISH VERBS and TENSES

The dictionary defines VERBS as the part of speech that expresses action, existence or occurrence. It comes from the Latin word *verbum* meaning word.

The three types of verbs are
1. Action Verbs
2. Linking Verbs and
3. Helping or Auxiliary Verbs

ACTION VERBS

Examples of Action verbs are eat, play, fight, and run.

John <u>eats</u> the apple.
Rahim and Aziz <u>play</u> soccer.
They <u>fight</u> in the street.
He <u>runs</u> in the field.

LINKING VERBS

Examples of Linking Verbs are verbs from "to be" is, are, was, were, has, and have.

Rita <u>is</u> happy.
They <u>are</u> in this room.
Rajan <u>has</u> a new bicycle.
Fatimah and Ahmad <u>have</u> a new baby.

HELPING OR AUXILIARY VERBS

Examples of these verbs are am, is, are was, were but they do not stand on their own. These must be followed by another verb + ing form.

> Johan is playing baseball.
> They were waiting here for some time.
> She was rushing home after school.
> Vincent and Ah Chong were playing badminton.

Verbs are also classified into **REGULAR** and **IRREGULAR** Verbs.

Regular verbs: Verbs ending with 'a,e,i,o,u.' add d to it to form the past tense,

> E,g share with 'd' added becomes   shared
> care   with 'd' added becomes   cared

Verbs ending with a consonant add 'ed' to it to form the past tense

> E.g   pour   with 'ed' added becomes poured
> admit with 'ed' admitted

In regular verbs the past tense form of the verb has either 'd' or 'ed' added to it.

Irregular verbs do not follow any fixed pattern when changed into past tense

E.g.   see   saw   seen

They <u>see</u> the stars.

They <u>saw</u> the stars.

They <u>have seen</u> the stars.

arise arose arisen

The people <u>arise</u> against the king.

The people <u>arose</u> against the king.

The people <u>have arisen</u> against the king.

eat   ate   eaten

Roshida <u>eats</u> apples everyday.

She <u>ate</u> apples yesterday.

She <u>has eaten</u> all the apples.

Below is a list of all irregular verbs in the present form past form and participle forms.

LIST OF IRREGULAR VERBS

Simple Form (Base)	Simple Form	Past Past	Simple Participle	Simple Past	Past Participle
be	was, were	been	lie	lay	lain
become	became	become	light	lit lighted	lit lighted
begin	began	begun	lose	lost	lost
bend	bent	bent	make	made	made
bite	bit	bitten	meet	met	met
blow	blew	blown	pay	paid	paid
break	broke	broken	put	put	put

bring	brought	brought	quit	quit	quit
broadcast	broadcast	broadcast	read	read	read
build	built	built	ride	rode	ridden
buy	bought	bought	ring	rang	rung
catch	caught	caught	rise	rose	risen
choose	chose	chosen	run	ran	run
come	came	come	say	said	said
cost	cost	cost	see	saw	seen
cut	cut	cut	sell	sold	sold
dig	dug	dug	send	sent	sent
do	did	done	set	set	set
draw	drew	drawn	shake	shook	shaken
drink	drank	drunk	shoot	shot	shot
drive	drove	driven	shut	shut	shut
eat	ate	eaten	sing	sang	sung
fall	fell	fallen	sit	sat	sat
feed	fed	fed	sleep	slept	slept
feel	felt	felt	slide	slid	slid
fight	fought	fought	speak	spoke	spoken
fly	flew	flown	spend	spent	spent
forget	forgot	forgotten	spread	spread	spread
forgive	forgave	forgiven	stand	stood	stood
freeze	froze	frozen	steal	stole	stolen
get	got	gotten(got)	stick	stuck	stuck
give	gave	given	strike	struck	struck
go	went	gone	swear	swore	sworn
grow	grew	grown	sweep	swept	swept
hang	hung	hung	swim	swam	swum
have	had	had	take	took	taken
hear	herd	herd	teach	taught	taught
hide	hid	hidden	tear	tore	torn
hit	hit	hit	tell	told	told
hold	held	held	think	thoughtt	thought
hurt	hurt	hurt	throw	threw	thrown

keep	kept	kept	understand	understood	understood
know	knew	known	upset	upset	upset
lay	laid	laid	wake	woke	woken
lead	led	led	wear	wore	worn
leave	left	left	win	won	won
lend	lent	lent	withdraw	withdrew	withdrew
let	let	let	write	wrote	written

A VERB can be a single word, two words or three words.

The boys play soccer. (singular word)

The boy is playing soccer. (two words)

The game will be played next week. (three words)

Sometimes, there can be four words in a verb.

They should have been sharing the books.

STATIVE VERBS. These are sometimes called **NONPROGRESSIVE VERBS.**

Such verbs are: like, need, hate, want, prefer, know, believe, love and understand.

They usually do not take a continuous or progressive form but there are exceptions to the rule.

E.g. I think that grammar is easy.
I am thinking that grammar is easy. INCORRECT
I am thinking about grammar right now. CORRECT

I <u>hear</u> a bird right now.
I <u>am hearing </u>a bird right now. INCORRECT

Raja Nordin <u>loves </u>Rohani.
Raja Nordin <u>is loving</u> Rohani. INCORRECT

TENSES: Basically there are THREE Tenses. **The Present, The Past and The Future Tenses.**

The **Present Tense** has a variation of Four Tenses.

They are:
1. The Simple Present Tense.
2. The Present Continuous Tense or The Present Progressive Tense.
3. The Present Perfect Tense.
4. The Present Perfect Continuous or Present Perfect Progressive Tense.

Eg. The Simple Present Tense

Rahim <u>plays</u> soccer for his school.
Ah May <u>eats</u> rice everyday.
They <u>write</u> in their diary daily.
Kassim <u>does </u>not <u>drive</u> the car.
<u>Do</u> you <u>share</u> the book with her?

The Present Continuous or Present Progressive Tense

Rahim <u>is playing</u> soccer for his school.
Ah May <u>is eating</u> rice everyday.
They<u> are writing</u> in their diary right now.
Kassim<u> is </u>not<u> driving </u>the car.
<u>Are </u>you <u>sharing </u>the book with her?

The Present Perfect Tense

Rahim <u>has played</u> soccer for his school.
Ah May <u>has eaten</u> rice.
They <u>have written</u> in their diary.
Kassim <u>has</u> not <u>driven</u> the car.
<u>Has</u> Kassim <u>driven</u> the car?

The Present Perfect Continuous or Present Perfect Progressive Tense.

Rahim <u>has been playing</u> since for his school.
Ah May <u>has been eating</u> rice since she was very young.
They <u>have been writing</u> in their diary daily.
You <u>have</u> not <u>been</u> <u>sharing</u> the book with her.
<u>Have</u> you <u>been sharing</u> the book with her?

The **Past Tense** also has four variations.

They Are: 1. The Simple Past Tense.
2. The Past Continuous or Past Progressive Tense.
3. The Past Perfect Tense.
4. The Past Perfect Continuous or Past Perfect Progressive Tense.

The Simple Past Tense:

Eg. Rajan <u>kicked</u> the ball into the goal.
He <u>took</u> the pen with him.
They <u>wrote</u> in the book.
Rahimah and Susan <u>did</u> not <u>complete</u> their homework.
<u>Have</u> they <u>completed</u> their homework?

The Past Continuous or Past Progressive Tenses.

Eg. Rajan <u>was kicking</u> the ball into the goal.
He <u>was taking</u> the pen with him.
They <u>were writing</u> in the book.
Rahimah and Susan <u>are</u> not <u>completing</u> their homework.
<u>Are</u> they <u>com pleting</u> their homework?

The Past Perfect Tense

Eg. Rajan <u>had kicked</u> the ball into the goal.
He <u>had taken</u> the pen with him.
They <u>had written</u> in the book.
Rahima and Susan <u>had</u> not <u>completed</u> their homework.
<u>Had</u> they <u>completed</u> their homework?

The Past Perfect Continuous or Past Perfect Progressive Tense

Eg. Rajan <u>had been kicking</u> the ball into the goal.
He <u>had been taking</u> the pen with him.
They <u>had been writing</u> in the book,.
Rahima and Susan <u>had</u> not <u>been completing</u> their homework.
<u>Had</u> they <u>been completing</u> their homework?

The **Future Tense** also has its variations. In the future tense we usually use will or shall before the verb. *Will* is usually used for oral or informal language while *shall* is used for formal or written language. There is however no fixed rule in modern English in the use of *will* and *shall*. These are helping verbs or auxiliary verbs or modals.

The **Future Tense**

Johan <u>will play</u> soccer for the state. (Simple Future)
She <u>will be playing</u> netball for the state. (Future Continuous)
Devan <u>will have finished</u> his assignment by Friday (Future Perfect)
Chitra <u>would have been finishing</u> her assignment by Friday. (Future Perfect Continuous)
They <u>would</u> not <u>have finished</u> by Friday. (Future Perfect in the negative)
<u>Will</u> they <u>have finished</u> the assignment by Friday? (Future perfect in the interrogative)

EXERCISES

Change the following **Regular** verbs into the appropriate tenses: [Answers in page 134]

Verb

Present	Past	Participle
Share	_____	_____
Scare	_____	_____
Dare	_____	_____
Enjoy	_____	_____
Surprise	_____	_____
Play	_____	_____
Want	_____	_____
Shout	_____	_____
Kill	_____	_____
Fill	_____	_____

Change the following **IRREGULAR** Verbs into their appropriate tenses: [Answers in page 134]

Verbs	Past Tense	Participle
Eat	_____	_____
Write	_____	_____
Arise	_____	_____
Awake	_____	_____
Draw	_____	_____
Swim	_____	_____
See	_____	_____
Drink	_____	_____
Break	_____	_____
Bite	_____	_____

EXERCISE 1

Fill in the Blanks with the correct present tense form of the verbs: [Answers for Exercise 1 - 5 in pages 135-136]

1. Babies _____ when they are hungry. (cry)

2. A parrot _____ a song. (sing)

3 Jayasinth _____ for her book. (search)

4. Rahman _____ his car very carefully. (drive)

5. They _____ in the river. (swim)

6. Children _____ to play in the rain. (like)

7. The workers _____ the fruit from the trees. (collect)

8. She _____ netball for her school. (play)

9. Water _____ along the hills. (flow)

10. They _____ the water from the hills. (get)

EXERCISE 2

Change all the above sentences (in Exercise 1) into the present continuous form.

EXERCISE 3

Change all the sentences into the present perfect tense.

EXERCISE 4

Change all the sentences in the future tense.

CHAPTER 3
ADJECTIVES

Types of Adjectives
Comparisons of Adjectives
Order of Adjectives
Adjective formation
Exercises

ADJECTIVES

An **ADJECTIVE** is defined as a word used with a noun to add something to its meaning. It is a describing word. The adjective gives more information about the noun it is associated with.

> Eg. My boyfriend is tall, dark and handsome.
> That car is in excellent condition.
> This chair is very comfortable.

TYPES OE ADJECTIVES

1. **Descriptive Adjectives:** clever, good, soft, old, young, red.

   Eg. The old man caught a bad cold.

2. **Adjectives of Quality:**

   (a) Definite eg. one, five, twenty.

   Eg. Both players scored two goals in the second half.

   (b) Indefinite eg. all, any, some, much, several.

   Eg. We met several soldiers who had met some worriers.

3. **Demonstrative Adjectives**
   This, that, those, yonder.

   Eg. This stone was found in those hills.

4. **Interrogative Adjectives**
   Which, where, who, what, when.

   Eg. Where did you get the book from?

5. **Distributive Adjective**
   each, every, either, neither

   Eg. Either he or you will have to answer.

Comparison of Adjectives

The **POSITIVE** is used when we describe one object.

   Eg. The tiger is a <u>big</u> animal.

The **COMPARATIVE** is used when we compare two objects. We add 'er' to the adjective. Eg. The elephant is <u>bigger</u> than a tiger.

The **SUPERLATIVE** is used when we talk about more than two objects. We add 'est' to the adjective. Eg. The whale is the <u>biggest</u> mammal.

These are degrees of comparisons of adjectives.

REGULAR ADJECTIVES

Positive	Comparative	Superlative
Big	Bigger	Bigest
Bold	Bolder	Boldest
Clever	Cleverer	Cleverest
Great	Greater	Greatest
Late	Later	Latest
Shallow	Shallower	Shallowest
Simple	Simpler	Simplest

IRREGULAR ADJECTIVES

Positive	Comparative	Superlative
beautiful	more beautiful	most beautiful
gracious	more gracious	most gracious
learned	more learned	most learned
ignorant	more ignorant	most ignorant
good	better	best

bad	worse	worst
much	more	most
many	more	most
little	less	least

ORDER OF ADJECTIVES

When two or more adjectives are used there is an order in which the adjectives are used:

Eg. He is a pleasant old man. Pleasant is opinion and old is fact.
He has bought a wonderful new car.
Rahim is an active young man.
That friendly old lady has gone to town.

The rule of Order of adjectives usually follows:

(a) Determiners like articles a, an, the.
(b) Opinion like beautiful, expensive or delicious.
(c) Size like length shape or width big, square or little.
(d) Age like old, young or antique.
(e) Colour like red, blue or green.
(f) Origin like French, Italian or Chinese.
(g) Material iron, wooden, silver or golden.
(h) Purpose like sports, village or football.
(i) Nouns like car, roses or house.

Examples of sentences showing order of adjectives:

1. I have a beautiful, old, French, Sports car.
2. That is an expensive, antique, silver chair.
3. She has a big, old, black dog.
4. She bought some gorgeous, red, natural flowers.

ADJECTIVE FORMATION

Prefixes	*Nouns*	*Adjectives*
-y	wealth	wealthy
-lee	time	timly
-al	profession	professional
-ial	industry	industrial
-ous	fame	famous
-ary	moment	momentary
-less	power	powerless
-ful	care	careful
-vie	completion	competitive

EXERCISE 1 [Answers in page 137]

Identify the adjectives in the following sentences:

    a. He is a man of few words.

    b. The ship sustained heavy damages.

    c. Zainal called over several times.

    d. Every dog has its day.

    e. A live ass is better than a dead lion.

    f. That boy is industrious.

    g. Which pen do you prefer?

    h. She preferred the red pen.

    i. That French Sports car is in excellent condition.

    j. They live in a comfortable home.

ADJECTIVE EXERCISES

EXERCISE 2 [Answers in page 137]

Supply suitable adjectives in the blanks at the following sentences:

1. The _____ prize was won by the _____ boy.

2. This is a very _____ matter.

3. The_____ woman lives in a wretched house.

4. It is a _____ lie.

5. The _____ man wants some help.

6. The _____ bird catches the worm.

7. It is better to be _____ than to be wealthy.

8. He always walks with a _____ step.

9. Every cloud has a _____ lining.

10 She was a lady of _____ ambition.

EXERCISE 3 [Answers in page 137]

Underline the adjectives in the following sentences:

1. The tall gentleman wore a blue shirt.

2. The beautiful lady wore a long gown.

3. The weather was wet and cloudy.

4. The ugly old woman spoke in a hoarse, cracked voice.

5. The lost ball was found near the garden gate.

6. Roshen drove the new car with great care.

7. Faizal bought a new silk shirt.

8. They went to the hill resort for a short holiday.

9. The newly established college had many new students.

10. They were given a serious warning.

CHAPTER 4
PRONOUNS

TYPES OF PRONOUNS - Personal Pronouns - Possessive Pronouns - Interrogative Pronouns - Reflexive Pronouns - Relative Pronouns - Demonstrative Pronouns Exercises

PRONOUNS

A **pronoun** is a word or form that substitutes for a noun.
Pro - for pronoun for a noun.

	SINGULAR	PLURAL
FIRST PERSON	I	we
SECOND PERSON	you	you
THIRD PERSON	he/she/it	they

TYPES OF PRONOUNS:

1. Personal Pronouns
2. Possessive Pronouns
3. Interrogative Pronouns
4. Reflexive Pronouns
5. Relative Pronouns
6. Demonstrative Pronouns
7. Indefinite Pronouns.

PERSONAL PRONOUNS

They are used either as a Subject or an Object of a verb

Subject	Object
I	me
you	you

he	him
she	her
it	it

Eg.   I saw her last week.
Rajan visited me yesterday.
We saw you last night.
She spoke to me last week.
We bought from them.

If the personal pronoun is a subject it comes before a verb.

If it is the object it is used after a verb or a preposition.

POSSESSIVE PRONOUN

Possessive pronouns differ from possessive adjectives.

Possessive pronouns	Possessive adjectives
mine	my
his	his
hers	her
ours	our
yours	your
theirs	their

Possessive pronouns are usually used at the end of a sentence while possessive adjectives are usually used before a noun.

Possessive Pronouns	Possessive Adjectives

Eg. This car is mine	This is my car.
That bicycle is his.	That is his bicycle.
That board is ours.	That is our board,
Those shirts are yours,	Those are your shirts.

INTERROGATIVE PRONOUNS

Interrogative pronouns are used to introduce questions. Words used at the beginning of a sentence are:

Who, what, which, when, whom, where and why.

Eg. Whose are these books?
Who met you there?
What page are we on?
Which road leads us there?
Why are you so late?
When do you hope to complete the work?

Note: All interrogative pronouns are immediately followed by a verb.

There will be a noun or pronoun after the verb.

REFLEXIVE PRONOUNS

I	-	myself	we	-	ourselves
you	-	yourself (singular)	you	-	yourselves (plural)
he	-	himself	they	-	themselves

she - herself	Raman and Ali - themselves
it - itself	
one - oneself	
Raman - himself	
Aminah - herself	

Eg. I washed the clothes myself.
You tied the knot yourself.
He cooks the meal himself.
She cleaned the plates herself.
It rinses the clothes itself.
Ahmad washed the car by himself.
Sharina polished the shoes by herself.

We washed the clothes ourselves.
You boys tied the knot yourselves.
They cooked the meals themselves.
They cleaned the plates themselves.
They rinse the clothes themselves.
Ahmad and Ali washed the car by themselves.
Sharina and Rohani polished the shoes themselves.

RELATIVE PRONOUNS

These are used to say something that describes the person or thing we are talking about.
The words who, whom, whose, which, where and that introduces a clause beginning with these relative pronouns.

Eg. I have a friend whose father owns a mini-market.

This is the shop that sells computer parts.

They have found the boy who lost his pen.

That is the book which has lost a page

There is the boy whose father helped me.

DEMONSTRATIVE PRONOUNS

This - these   That - those   are   examples   of Demonstrative Pronouns.

'this' and 'that' are Singular while 'these' and 'those' are plural.

Eg. This is my house.
  These are our books.
  That horse is pretty.
  Those horses are healthy.

INDEFINITE PRONOUNS

Anyone, someone, anybody, somebody, everybody and nobody are examples of indefinite pronouns. Indefinite pronouns are used when we are not referring any particular person or thing.

Anything something and everything are also examples of indefinite pronouns.

Eg. Is anyone there?

Has anybody seen my book?

Someone is at the door.

Everyone can solve that problem.

Are there enough chairs for everybody?

None *and one are also indefinite pronouns.*

EXERCISE 1 [Answers in page 138]

Underline the correct relative pronoun in the following sentences:

1. The answer which you gave me is incorrect.

2. We met the sailors whose ship was wrecked

3. The cat killed the rat which ate the food.

4. This is the house that his father built.

5. The book that you gave me is a very new one.

6. Pass me the letters that the postman brought

7. Here is the book that you lent me.

8. I know the lady whose house was burgled

9. They had children who were cruel.

10. Children whose parents are kind grow up to be good.

EXERCISE 2 [Answers in page 138]

Choose the correct pronoun in each of the sentences:

1. It was (he/him) (who/ whom) we saw in the shop.

2. (He/Him) and (I/me) went for a walk.

3. No one saw (she/her). Everyone thinks it was (I/me)

4. (He/ She) and you sing very well together.

5. Let you and (I/me) go to the shore.

6. The matter must remain a secret between you and (I/me).

7. It appears to be (they/them).

8. I spoke to (he/him) and (she/her).

9. Mary and (I/me) saw the ship in the horizon.

10. (Who/Whom) do you think we met?

EXERCISE 3 [Answers in page 138]

Fill in the blanks with suitable relative pronouns.

1. I do not know the man _____ hit the boy.

2. He _____ is merciful shall meet mercy.

3. The letter _____ you wrote never arrived.

4. You have not brought the book _____ I asked for.

5. Listen to _____ I say.

6. He plays the game _____ he likes best.

7. It is an ill wind _____ blows nobody any good.

8. He is the very man _____ we want.

9. She has gone to Ipoh _____ is her birth place.

10. God helps _____ who help themselves.

CHAPTER 5
PREPOSITIONS

Types of Prepositions - Preposition of Time - Preposition of place - Preposition of Manner - Preposition of Cause or Reason - Preposition of Purpose - Preposition of Possession- Preposition of Measure - Preposition of influence, motive, source or origin. Exercises.

PREPOSITION

The word preposition means 'that which is placed before'. A preposition is a word placed before a noun or a pronoun to show the relationship between a person or a thing.

Generally there are three types of prepositions. They are:

1. Simple prepositions like at, in, on, from, out, with and through.

    Eg. They live at Pearl Gardens, Ipoh.
         The books are in the cupboard.
         The glasses are on the table.
         You cannot play badminton with the broken racquet.
         They walked through the door.

2. Compound Prepositions like around, above, beyond, inside and outside.

    Eg. The children walked around the fire.
         The aeroplane flew above the clouds.
         The students stayed inside the classroom.
         The girls went outside to play.

3. Phrasal or Prepositions in group of words or phrases.

    Eg. According to the instructions you must complete this work today.
         She disagreed with my suggestion.

The following are commonly used prepositions;

according to	afflict with	agree to (something)
agree with (somebody)	angry with	ashamed of
attack on	blame for	change for (something)
change with (somebody)	comment on	
complain of	confer with	conscious
defiance of	despair of	die of
differ from (opinion)	differ with (somebody)	disappointed in (something)
disappointed with (somebody)	disgusted at (something)	disgusted with (somebody)
dislike for	divide among (many)	divide between (two)
equal to	filled with	full of
good for	guilty of	indignant at (something)
indignant with (somebody)	inspired by	interfere with
invasion of	meddle with	opposite of
part from (somebody)	part with (something)	prevail on
protest against	pursuit of	recoil from
regard for	rely on	similar to
suffer from	tired of (something)	tired with (action)
thirst for (or after)	vexed at (something)	vexed with (somebody)
victim of	wait for (person/ thing)	wait upon (somebody)
write about (something)	write to (somebody)	

TYPES OF PREPOSITIONS

Preposition of Time:

After, at, before, behind, and during.

> Eg. They arrived before dinner.
> We had our tea during the break.

Preposition of place:

about, across, among, on, in, up, towards and under

> Eg. They placed among the books.
> The crowd walked towards the station.

Preposition of Manner:

by, with and through

> Eg. Jack walked by without seeing us.
> They went through the notes very carefully.

Preposition of Cause, reason or purpose:

for, of, from and through

> Eg. He lost his wallet through carelessness.
> In the cold weather she shivered with fever.

Preposition of possession:

by, of, with

> Eg They walked there with their equipment.
> Birds of a feather flock together.

Preposition of measure, standard, rate or value:

by and at

> Eg. Janila was taller than her sister by two inches.
> We were carefully watching at the wall clock.

Preposition of contrast or similarity

for and after

> Eg. For all his wealth he is not happy.
> After every effort one may fail

Preposition of inference, motive, source or origin.

from

> Eg. Light emanates from the sun.
> Contentment is obtained from good health.

EXERCISE 1

Fill in the blanks with suitable prepositions. [Answers in page 139]

1. Christmas falls _____ December.

2. She received a present _____ Sabrina.

3. Rohani is _____ two inches taller than her sister.

4. We have been living in Pearl Gardens _____ six years.

5. They have been living in Ruby Gardens _____ 1957.

6. They did not see the cat because it was _____ the bed.

7. Jasmine ran _____ the stairs and opened the door.

8. Stephen received a letter _____ from his uncle yesterday.

9. They lent a book _____ Johari.

10. Devan borrowed some money _____ Rajan.

Exercise 2

Underline the preposition in the following sentences:
[Answers in page 139]

1   You cannot play badminton with that broken racquet.

2   She looked for her watch but could not find it.

3. The plan consisted of three stages.

4. We looked at a lot of books but did not buy any.

5. My sister has applied to join this university.

6. If you ask for some money nobody will give any.

7. You should not ask about his father. He will get upset.

8. The government is going to pay for the new stadium.

9. Why don't you talk to the teacher about this idea?

10. Where do I start from?

CHAPTER 6
ADVERBS

ADVERBS

An adverb is a word that modifies a verb, an adjective or another adverb.

An adverb usually helps to answer the question why, where, when or how something is done. Usually when '+ly' is added to an adjective the word becomes an adverb but this is not always the case. Eg. quick becomes quickly and slaw becomes slowly.

TYPES OF ADVERBS

Adverbs of time:

Already, before, since, seldom and some are examples of these.

>   Eg. The tourists have already left the country.
>   They have visited this place before.

Adverbs of Place:

here, there, everywhere and nowhere

>   Eg. The children have come here before.
>   They have littered the place everywhere.

Adverbs of manner:

Badly, slowly, easily and well are some examples.

Eg. They have slowly built up the temple.
The wall was easily broken.

Adverbs of Number:

Examples of these are once, twice, often and frequently.

Eg. The students came here frequently.
They often go to the cinema.

Adverbs of Reason:

Hence and therefore are some examples of these adverbs

Eg. We left the class early. Therefore, we were able to go for the show.
The fruit is ripe, hence, there are many ants on the tree.

Adverbs of Degree:

Almost, any, quite, very, much and rather are some examples.

Eg. The students are very disappointed.
The children would rather stay at home.

Interrogative or Question Adverbs:

Where, when, why and how are some examples of these.

Eg. Where did the aeroplane fly?
How did the piglet control the plane?

Adverbs of Affirmation or negation:

Some examples of these are yes, certainly, no and not.

> They certainly plucked some rambutans.
> We definitely did not.

In the expression of degrees in adverbs we usually add 'more' to the positive to make it comparative and 'most' to make the superlative.

Positive	Comparative	Superlative
happily	more happily	most happily
slowly	more slowly	most slowly
carefully	more carefully	most carefully

EXERCISE 1

Underline the adverbs and tell the types of adverbs identified. [Answers in page 140]

1. We have met them in the park once or twice.

2. She rose up very early.

3. The bus station is very far off.

4. They have gone away from here.

5. The patient is much worse today.

6. We were very kindly received.

7. He arrived a few minutes ago.

8. Peter is old enough to know better.

9. Too many cooks spoil the broth.

10. We surely expect them tomorrow.

EXERCISE 2

Underline the adverbs in the following sentences and say what type of adverb it is. [Answers in page 140]

1. The pineapples were quite good.

2. I once saw him play a birdie at golf.

3. Where did you place the book?

4. Wisdom is too high for a fool.

5. I wonder why you never told me.

6. Sabrina sees things differently now.

7. I would rather not visit him.

8. Do not crowd your work so close together.

9. I have heard this before.

10. There is a screw loose somewhere.

CHAPTER 7
CONJUNCTIONS

Types of Conjunctions
Conjunctions of Time - Conjunctions of
Cause or Reason - Conjunctions of
Purpose - Conjunctions of Condition -
Conjunctions of Reason or consequence
- conjunction of concession -
conjunction of comparison
Exercises

CONJUNCTIONS

A conjunction is a joiner. It is a word that connects (conjoins) parts of a sentence.

Simple little conjunctions are called CO-ORDINATING CONJUNCTIONS.

Examples of these are and, but, or, yet, for and so.

Other conjunctions are SUBORDINATE and CORRELATIVE CONJUNCTIONS.

Examples of subordinate conjunctions are:

> After, although, as if, before, even though, if, once, since, than, that, though, till, unless, when, whenever, whereas are examples of subordinate conjunctions.

Subordinate conjunctions are of many types:

1. **Time**

   Eg. I returned home after she had gone.

2. **Cause or Reason**

   Eg. As she was not there I spoke to her brother.

3. **Purpose**

   Eg. We ate that we may be healthy and strong.

4. Condition

Eg.   He will go if his brother goes.

5. Result or Consequence

Eg.   James was so tired that he could hardly walk.

Related conjunctions are used in pairs.

6. Concession

Eg.   She will not see him though he comes.

7. Comparison

Eg.   June is taller than her sister Jane.

CORRELATED CONJUNCTIONS

Correlated conjunctions are used in pairs to show the relationship between an idea expresses in different parts of a sentence.

Examples:

both	and	and
not only		but also
neither		nor
either		or
whether		or

Eg. They worked hours in order that they may complete their work on time.

You may borrow the book provided that you will return it nect week.

EXERCISE 1

Point out the conjunctions in the following sentence and identify the type of conjunction. [Answers in page 141]

1. You will be late unless you hurry.

2. He asked if we might have a holiday.

3. Ann will not succeed if she does not work hard.

4. Since you say so, I must believe it.

5. Roshen deserves to succeed since he worked hard.

6. Either you are mistaken or I am.

7. Unless you tell me the truth I shall punish you.

8. Johan waited till the bus arrived.

9. The soldiers abandoned their post lest they be killed.

10. Blessed are the merciful for they shall obtain mercy.

EXERCISE 2

Fill in the blanks with either and or but: [Answers in page 141]

1. John didn't study for the test _____ Sabrina did.

2. Johan lives in the hostel _____ Devan lives at home.

3. Both Rohani _____ Rohana live in the hostel.

4. Jack isn't here today _____ Linda isn't here either.

5. Susan will not be at the meeting tonight _____ I will be there.

6. Rahaman _____ Jamilah arrived with their friends.

7. I will be there _____ she will not come.

8. Nirmalah went home early _____ got ready to go for games.

9. Love is blind _____ but the neighbours are not.

10. All of them went inside the boat _____ was left behind.

CHAPTER 8

INTERJECTION

Types of Interjection - Interjection of Joy - Interjection of Grief - Interjection of Surprise - Interjection of Approval.

INTERJECTIONS

An Interjection also known as EXCLAMATION is used to express a sudden feeling or emotion 'Ah!', 'Alas!', 'Hello!' 'Hurrah!' and 'Ouch' are examples of exclamation or interjections.

The can be classified into:-

1   Joy   eg. hurrah! 'great!'.

2. Grief   eg. 'alas!'.

3. Surprise or shock   eg. 'what!'

4. Approval   eg. 'well done!'

An interjection is sometimes expressed as a single word or a non-sentence phrase followed by the punctuation mark ' ! '.

Interjections are usually placed at the beginning of a sentence.

   Eg. Cheers!   Excuse me!   Beg your pardon!
     Hey that's mine!
     Goodbye!
     'Hurrah'. And 'Ouch' are a few examples of it.

They can be classified into:—

1. Interjection of Joy   eg. Hurrah!
2. Interjection of Grief   eg. Alas!

3. Interjection of Surprise or shock   eg. What!
4. Interjection of Approval   eg. Well done!

An Interjection is sometimes expressed as a single word or non-sentence phrase followed by a punctuation mark!. They are usually placed at the beginning of a sentence.

Eg. Goodbye!
    Cheers!
    Excuse me!
    Beg your pardon!
    Hey, that's mine!

CHAPTER 9
ARTICLES

The Indefinite Articles
The Definite Articles
Zero Articles or Omission of Articles
Exercises

ARTICLES

An **Article** is a word that is used to indicate a type of reference made by the noun. Articles can be:

(a) indefinite
(b) definite or
(c) zero article where no article is used

The vowel spelling sounds 'a' 'e' 'i' 'o' and 'u' usually use a or an before the article.

It must be emphasized that this use is based on the pronunciation of the word and not on the spelling of the word.

THE INDEFINITE ARTICLE

The use of a or an before the noun makes the article an indefinite article. They are usually

Eg. a book   a cat   an accident
     a school   an elephant   an actor
     an accountant   an enemy   an interesting game
     an umbrella   a leaner driver   an L-driver
     a straight road   an S-Bend

Other examples of indefinite articles are:

        an heir   an hour   an honour
        an honest person

Note these words start with a silent 'h' but are still nouns starting with a vowel sound.

Words like a union, a uniform, a university and a European do not start with a vowel sound when written but with a vowel sound when pronounced.

USAGE OF A/an:

1. When something is mentioned for the first time 'a' is used.

   Eg. She took a book from the shelf.

2. 'A' or 'an' is also used to refer to a person's religion, class, or character.

   Eg. He is a Christian.
       She is an understanding person.

3. It is also used to refer to a person's occupation.

   Eg. He is an accountant. She is a nurse.

4. A or an is used to mean each.
   Eg. He goes to the library once a week.

THE DEFINITE ARTICLE

'The' is the definite article

1. When we refer to a particular person or a specific object we use 'the'.

   Eg. This is <u>the</u> car tat I want to sell.

2. We use 'the' when we refer to the same thing again.

   Eg. I bought a book. <u>The</u> book cost me RM 50.00

3. 'The' is used for a noun where there is only one.

   Eg. <u>The</u> king visited St. Johns Park yesterday.

4. 'The' is used with the following expressions.

the west	the moon	the sun	the climate
the king	the climate		
the first	the earth	the begining	the top
the end	the sultan		

5. We use 'the' before superlatives.

   Eg. Johan is <u>the</u> most intelligent student in the class.

6. We use 'the' before first second third fourth or the last.

   Eg. This is <u>the</u> first time he is coming here.

7. We use 'the' before names of rivers, seas, oceans, gulfs, canals, deserts or mountain ranges.

   Eg. <u>The</u> Persian Gulf is a very dangerous area for ships.

8 'The' is used for countries which include the word Republic.

   Eg. There is always unrest in the Republic of Congo.

9. 'The' is used before a singular noun that stands for a whole class.

   Eg. The Rose is a sweet smelling flower.

10. We use 'the' before musical instruments when it is used after the verbs yo play or to learn.

    Eg. Janet knows how to play <u>the</u> flute.

11. 'The' is used to refer to a class of people. <u>The</u> handicapped are safe.

12. We use 'the' when we refer collectively to a race or group of people.

    Eg. The Rohingya are an unfortunate people.

ZERO ARTICLES or OMISSION OF THE ARTICLE

1. No articles are used before uncountable nouns used in a general sense.

    Eg. Money does give one happiness.

2. No articles are used before plural nouns used in a general sense.

    Eg. Motor cars are very costly nowadays.

3. No articles are used with words such as school, prison, church, home, town, college.

    Eg. They are going home after college.

4. No articles are used when we mention games.

    Eg. They play soccer.

5. When we talk about meals we do not use articles.

    Eg. We have breakfast at six in the morning.

6. We do not use articles before names of towns, state or city unless it is used as an adjective.

    Eg. She comes from Ipoh.

7. Articles are not used, before names of roads, streets except when the road or street joins two places.

    Eg. Pearl Avenue is in Ipoh.

8. No articles are used before abstract nouns.

   Eg. Love is blind but the neighbours are not.

9. Articles are not used before names of many countries.

   Eg. They are going to Japan.

10. No articles are used before such diseases as malaria, tuberculosis, influenza or cholera.

   Eg. The young children are infected with malaria.

EXERCISE 1 [Answers in page 142]

Fill in the Blanke with 'A' "an' or 'the'

1. Copper is _____useful metal.

2. _____ able man has not always a distinguished look.

3. _____ Reindeer is _____ native of Norway.

4. I first met him _____ year ago.

5. She has come without _____ umbrella.

6. The children found _____ egg in the nest.

7. Let us discuss _____ matter seriously.

8. _____ lion is _____ king of the beasts.

9. If you see him give him _____ message.

10. He is _____ honour to his profession.

EXERCISE 2 [Answers in page 142]

Insert articles where necessary:

1. Sun rises in East.

2. The brave soldier lost arm in battle.

3. River was spanned by iron bridge.

4. He likes to picture himself original thinker.

5. I have not seen him since he was child.

6. Children suffered from malaria.

7. Trip to Japan was arranged week ago.

8. Livingstone was great explorer.

9. We started late in afternoon.

10. My favourite flower is rose.

CHAPTER 10
GERUNDS AND INFINITIVES

The GERUND is a non-finite verb form used to make a verb phrase that can serve in Place of a noun phrase.

Gerunds end in (-ing)

eg. play - playing   enjoy - enjoying

A verb + ing usually becomes a gerund. When we use a verb form in -ing more like a noun it is usually a gerund.

Eg. Playing soccer is fun.
    Swimming is my favourite hobby.
    Fishing in the hot sun is tiring.

INFINITIVES [To + verb (base)]

These are formed with "to" in front of the verb. Eg. to walk, to play, to eat.

Note infinitives will not have past tense of the verb after it,

Infinitives can be subject of a sentence:

Eg. To write in French is difficult
    To love someone is a wonderful feeling.
    To go to school is enjoyable.

Infinitives can be object of a verb:

Eg. I like to write in Spanish.
    I hope to pass the examination this time.
    It is important to practice speaking in English.

The word 'to' is frequently used with the infinitive.

After words like let, make, dare, see or hear we do not use an infinitive.

> Eg. I will not let you go.
>   You dare not do it.

EXERCISE 1 [Answers in page 143]

Identify the gerunds in the following sentences and say whether they are the subject or object of the verb.

1. Hearing the noise we went to the door.

   _____

2. Walking on the grass is not allowed.

   _____

3. The old lady hated spending money.

   _____

4. We spent the afternoon playing in the field.

   _____

5. Praising all alike is praising none.

   _____

6. Singing to herself was her delight.

   _____

7. Standing on his head is a difficult task for him.

   _____

8. Jumping over the fence the thief escaped.

   _____

9. Success is not merely winning applause.

   _____

10. Reading small print has ruined his eyes.

   _____

EXERCISE 2 [Answers in page 143]

Fill in the blanks with infinitives where necessary.

1. The Captain ordered his soldiers_____ march forward,

2. The fruit is fit _____ eat.

3. I was sorry _____ hear that.

4. _____ advance was difficult _____ retreat was impossible.

5. Everybody wants _____ be happy.

6. It is delightful _____ hear the sound of waves.

7. He hesitated _____ tell the story.

8. I wish _____ see you again.

9. He has the power _____ concentrate his thought.

10. He wanted _____ go swimming in the rover.

CHAPTER 11
SENTENCES

Types and Analysis - The
Alphabet -words - phrases
- clauses and sentences.
Sentences-Statement - Question-
Request, Command or Order and
Exclamations. Simple, complex and
compound sentences. Exercises.

The alphabet has 26 letters in the English Language. A, b, d and t are letters. A thought which combines a few letters makes a word.

E,g cat is a word 'I' and 'a' are single letters which are considered as a word.

When a few words are put together they become a phrase, a clause or a sentence.

A phrase is a group of words in a sentence that has no verb,

e.g. 'on the table' and 'in the cupboard'.

A clause on the other hand is a group of words in a sentence that contains a verb.

e.g. 'placed on the table' and 'written on the paper'.

A sentence is a group of words arranged in a logical manner to make a complete thought.

A. Sentences ban be:

1. a statement
   e,g. The earth revolves round the sun.

2. a question
   e.g. Have you seen the sunset?

3. a request, command or an order
   e.g. Put the gun down now.

4. an exclamation

    e.g. What! Is that gun loaded!

B. The sentence can be:-

1. Simple

    e.g. I have a cat.

2. Complex

    e.g. I have a cat which is very friendly.

3. Compound

    e.g. I have a cat and it is very friendly.

Go. Is the shortest sentence in the English language. The Subject is (You) understood and the verb is go.

PHRASES

Some examples of phrases are: 'on the table', 'of few words' and 'with great speed'.

Phrases can be adjectival, adverbial or noun depending on their function

The church stood <u>on the hill</u>. This is a noun phrase.

He drove his car <u>with great speed</u>. This is an adverbial phrase.

He is a <u>man of caliber</u>. This is an adjectival phrase.

CLAUSES

Clauses are either main or subordinate clauses. The main clause is independent while the subordinate clause is dependent on the main clause.

> e.g. I went to the school which stood on the hill. 'I went to the school' is the main clause.
> 'which stood on the hill' is the subordinate clause.

He drove his car maneuvering it with great speed. 'He drove his car' is the main clause 'maneuvering it with great speed' is the subordinate clause.

> Eg He is a man who has great caliber. 'He is a man' is the main clause. 'who has great caliber' is the subordinate clause.

Subordinate clauses can be noun or adjective or adverb clauses depending on their function.

> e.g. I am sure that I will get a prize. 'that I will get a prize" is a noun clause.

That is the repair that was badly needed. 'that was badly needed' is an adjective clause.

I want you to wait here until he returns. 'wait here until he returns' is an adverbial clause.

SENTENCES

A sentence has a subject and a predicate. The boy walked to school 'The boy' is the subject and 'walked to school' is the predicate.

SIMPLE SENTENCES

A sentence that has a subject and a predicate is called the simple sentence. It has only one finite verb. Here are some examples of simple sentences:

1. He stole my wallet.
2. The man stood at the door.
3. He opened the cupboard.
4. That lady wore a red dress.
5. The boy has hurt his foot.

COMPLEX SENTENCES

A complex sentence consists of one main clause and one or more subordinate clauses.

The subordinate clause is usually introduced by a relative pronoun.

> e.g. I went to a school which stood on a hill.
> 'I went to a school' is the main or independent clause.
> 'which stood on a hill' is the subordinate or dependant clause.

Here are some examples of complex sentences:

1. This is the man who stole my wallet.
2. The man stood at the door which was open.
3. He opened the cupboard which had plenty of books.
4. The lady who wore a red dress sat next to me.
5. The boy who has hurt his foot cannot walk.

COMPOUND SENTENCES

A compound sentence has two ideas or two main clauses joined together by a co-coordinating conjunction.

e.g.   I went to a school and it stood on a hill.

'I went to a school' is the main clause and 'it stood on a hill' is another main clause.

Here are some examples of compound sentences.

1. This is the man and he stole my wallet.
2. The man stood at the door and it was open.
3. He opened the cupboard but there were no books in it.
4. The lady wore a red dress and she sat next to me.
5. The boy has hurt his foot and he cannot walk.

EXERCISE 1 [Answers in page 144]

Identify if the sentence is a statement, question, request or an exclamation.

1. Kuala Lumpur is the capital city of Malaysia. _____

2. Where does he live? _____

3. Oh! They live in a cave. _____

4. Please turn off the fan. _____

5. When do you hope to finish those exercises? _____

6. Ouch! The pin has pricked my finger. _____

7. The sun rises in the East. _____

8. The earth revolves round the sun._____

9. Oh! The earth is rotating on its axis. _____

10. There are twelve months in a year._____

EXERCISE 2 [Answers in page 144]

Identify the phrases in the following sentences and say what type they are.

1. The magistrate was a <u>man with a kind heart</u>.

   _____

2. Johan answered <u>in a rude manner</u>.

   _____

3 .I should hate to do <u>such a thing</u>.

   _____

4. The chief lived in a <u>house built of stone</u>.

   _____

5. Jasen is coming <u>at this very moment</u>.

   _____

6. He refuses to answer <u>that silly question</u>.

   _____

7. He took the book <u>with no writing in it</u>.

   _____

8. The arrow fell <u>on this very spot</u>.

   _____

9. Horses prefer living <u>in dark stables</u>.

   _____

10. He is a man <u>without a friend</u>.

   _____

EXERCISE 3 [Answers in page 144]

Identify the clauses in the following sentences and say what type they are:

1. He behaves as one might expect him to do.

   _____

2. When he returned we asked him many questions.

   _____

3. He saw the clock that had stopped.

   _____

4. They went where living was cheaper.

   _____

5. When he entered the room he saw the mirror broken.

   _____

6. She wanted to know how far it was.

   _____

7. She took a lamp with her because the night was dark.

   _____

8. I think you have made a mistake.

   _____

9. They may go home after the work is finished.

   _____

10. If you do not hurry you will miss the train.

   _____

EXERCISE 4 [Answers in page 145]

Join each pair of sentences into complex sentences.

Do not use 'and', 'but' or 'so'.

1. The book belongs to Ramlah. It is a red one.

   _____

2. The woman was selling flowers. She stood at the corner of the street.

   _____

3. The girl fell heavily. The girl hurt herself.

   _____

4. The teacher praised the girls. They had worked hard.

   _____

5. I visited the little cottage. I was born in it.

   _____

6. I was gazing out of the window. I saw a crowd.

   _____

7. Stephen was riding a horse. It looked tired.

   _____

8. The old man went to the doctor. The doctor stayed next door.

   _____

9. The horse fell. It was pulling a heavy load.

_____

10. The man caught a fish. He took it home.

_____

EXERCISE 5 [Answers in page 145]

Change the following Complex sentences into Simple sentences.

1. Please tell me which way the wind is blowing.

   _____

2. They heard the news that he was saved.

   _____

3 We saw them when the clock struck six.

   _____

4. I admit that I have made a mistake.

   _____

5. She is a lady who is very intelligent.

   _____

6. I can tell you how old she is.

   _____

7. They all believed the story the traveler told.

   _____

8. Jason lives in a house that is very big.

   _____

9. They asked me where I lived.

   _____

10. Roshen lost his ticket because he was careless.

   _____

CHAPTER 12

DIRECT AND INDIRECT SPEECHES

General Rules to be followed
when changing direct to indirect
speech/ Exercises.

Direct Speech is the speech or saying exactly what someone has said. It is also known as quoted speech. The speech is usually word for word and it appears with quotation marks which are "open inverted commas at the beginning and closed inverted commas at the end. "

Eg. Stephen says, "I am hungry."
When changed into indirect speech it becomes
Stephen says that he was hungry.

When we report what was said without quoting the actual words it becomes indirect or reported speech.

Eg. Hamdan said, "I am very happy now.".
Hamdan said that he was very happy then.

When we change the direct into indirect speech the following rules have to be followed:

1. The verb in the simple present becomes the simple past.

Eg.   He said, "I am thirsty."
He said that he was thirsty.

2. The verb in the present continuous becomes past continuous.

Eg.   He said," My teacher is writing letters."
He said his teacher was writing letters.

3. The present perfect becomes the past perfect.

   Eg.   Suresh said, "I have passed the examination."
         Suresh said that he had passed the examination

4. Sometimes the past tense remains unchanged to express the correct meaning.

   Eg.   Hashim said, "I lived six years in Indonesia."
         Hashim said that he lived six years in Indonesia.
         Hashim said that he had lived six years in Indonesia.

5. Pronouns I, You, he/she, we, my and our change.

   Eg.   He said. "I must go."
         He said that he must go.
         She told the boy, "We know your sister."
         She told the boy that they knew his sister.

6. Other words that change are:

ago	becomes	before.
here		there
this		that
these		those
now		then
today		the next day
yesterday		the previous day
last night		the night before
last week		the week before

EXERCISE 1 [Answers in page 146]

Change the following sentences into the indirect speech.

1. "Sit down boys," said the teacher.

2. He told the servant, "Hurry up and don't waste any time."

3. "Halt!" shouted the captain to his men.

4. "That is my new house." he told his friend.

5. She wrote, "I am waiting for my son's return."

6. "Are you coming home with me?" his father asked.

7. "Which way did the puppy go?" asked the man.

8. "What a stupid fellow you are!" he angrily remarked.

9. Anuar said "Oh! That is a nuisance."

10. "Don't you know the way home?" I asked.

EXERCISE 2 [Answers in page 146]

Change the following sentences into direct speech.

1. He said that the dog had died the previous night.

2. He told me that he was getting tired then.

3. Anuar ordered Rahim to get out of his sight.

4. She shouted to them to let her go.

5. Zahara claimed that she was very clever.

6. Rajan said that he wanted become a doctor.

7. He said that we are all sinners.

8. She said that good deeds washed away sins,

9. The boys asked which was the proper way to answer the questions.

10. He asked her what she wanted.

CHAPTER 13
ACTIVE AND PASSIVE VOICE

Sentences in active voice
Sentences in passive voice
Exercises

ACTIVE AND PASSIVE VOICE

In most sentences in English the subject performs the action denoted by the verb.

Amanda mailed the letter. When we write this in the passive it becomes The letter was mailed by Amanda. The subject is 'Amanda' and the object is "letter". In the active we put the subject first and the object last.

The active voice is so called because the person denoted by the subject acts.

In the passive form the object comes first and the subject becomes an agent.

The passive is so called because the person or thing denoted by the subject is not active or receives some action. Note, only transitive verbs can be used in the passive.

Eg. Colourful birds live in the rain forest.

This sentence cannot be changed into the passive because the sentence has no direct object. However, if you want to change in the passive you can say 'The rainforest is inhabited by colourful birds'.

EXERCISE 1 [Answers in page 147]

Change the following sentences into the passive voice.

1. The police caught the thief.

2. The dog bit the boy.

3. The cat killed the mouse.

4. The loud noise frightened the horses.

5. His father will write a letter.

6. He made a very remarkable recovery.

7. My cousin drew that picture.

8. The farmer gathers the harvest.

9. The men cut down the trees.

10. Christopher Columbus discovered America in 1492.

EXERCISE 2 [Answers in page 147]

Change the following sentences into the active voice

1. Not a word was spoken by Arshad.

2. She was praised by her teacher.

3. The teacher was pleased with the girl's work.

4. The town was destroyed by fire.

5. She was taken to the hospital by her friends.

6. The streets were lined with students.

7. The trees were blown down by the wind.

8. The child was knocked down by the car.

9. The sultan was welcomed by the people.

10. *Cry of the Graves* was written by Khalil Gibran.

CHAPTER 14
DERIVATIONS— PREFIXES AND SUFFIXES

DERIVATION

PREFIXES AND SUFFIXES

Derivation is the process of forming a new word on the basis of an existing word.

Eg.   happy - unhappy   or   happiness.

'happy' is the root word unhappy 'un' is the prefix. The meaning is now changed to not happy while in happiness 'ness' is the sufix which changes it into a noun from adjective 'happy' into happiness.

Below are listed some derivatives their meanings and examples:

Derivatives	Meanings	Examples
aqua	water	aquatic, aqueduct
audio	sound or hearing	audiotape, audio-visual-aids
capio	take	capture, captive
centum	a hundred	century, centenarian
clamo	shout or a loud noise	clamour, proclaim
creo	create	creature, creation
decem	ten	*December, decimal
emperor	command	emperor, empire

finis	end	final, finite
fotis	strong	fort, fortified
homo	man	human, homicide
liber	free	liberal, liberty
malus	bad	malice, maltreat
manus	hand	manual, manufacture
mitto	send	missile, mission
navis	a ship	navy, navigate
nova	nine	*November, nine
octa	eight	*October, octagon
pello	drive	expel, propel
pendeo	hang	depend, suspend
pes	foot	pedal, pedestrian
planus	level	plain, plan
porto	carry	import, potable
primus	first	primitive, primary
pro	before	pronoun. Prospect
quadro	four	quarter, quadrangle
quint	five	quintet, quinary

rego	rule	regal, regiment
rota	a wheel or round	rotation, rotate
septa	seven	*September, septagon
scribo	write	scripiure, manuscript
specio	see	spectacle, aspect
teneo	hold	contain, retain
unus	one	unit, union
vanus	empty	vanish, vain
vanio	come	venture, adventure
video	see	vision, video gram
vinco	overcome	victory, convince
voco	call	voice, vocal
volvo	roll	evolve, volume

* September   October   November   December

In actual fact September is the ninth month of the year yet it is called 'septa' meaning seventh.

Similarly October is the tenth month of the year yet 'octa' stands for eight.

November is the eleventh month of the year yet it is called 'nova' meaning nine.

December is the twelfth month of the year yet it is called 'dece' meaning ten.

This is because originally there were only ten months in a year beginning in March. Therefore, September, October, November and December were the seventh, eighth, ninth and tenth months

For in the beginning they had had a year of tenth months only. It was later in the 7th Century 673 B.C. that the Roman Ruler Numa Pompilius added January and February to the calendar making it twelve months in a year.

SUFFIXES

A suffix is an affix which is placed after a stem or root of the word. It is also known as a postfix. Suffixes change the meaning of the root word.

A suffix is an ending that is added to a base word to form a new word.

Suffix	Meaning	Examples
-able, -ible	capable of being	enable, capable, edible
-ain, -an	connected	maintain, publican
-ance, -ence	state of	repentance, existence
-ant	person	assistant, servant
-el, -et, ette	small	satchel, locket, cigarette
-ation	state	limitation, reservation
-er, -eer	person	teacher, engineer
-ess	female	waitress, princess
-fy	to make	simplify, modify
-icle, -sel	small	particle, morsel
-ist	person	typist, communist
-less	without	careless, fearless
-ling	little	darling, gosling

-ment	state of being	government, enjoyment
-ock	little	hillock, hammock
-oon, -on	large	balloon, gallon
-ous	full of	famous, glorious
-ism	condition or state	socialism, communism
-dom	condition	kingdom, freedom
-ship	condition or state	friendship, membership
-ize, -ise	make	capitalize, summarize
-ic	having the quality	democratic, fantastic
-ly	in the manner of	slowly, softly

Suffixes ending in parts of speech:

Nouns: -ence, -ance -or, -er, -ism, -ist, -ness, -ment, -ant, -ling, -ment, -ock, -ship, -ain, -an

Verbs: -ise, -ate, -fy, -en, -in, -ify

Adjectives: -able, -ible, -less, -ig, -icle, -ish, -ive, -ory, -ous

Adverbs: -ice, -ily, -ly

APPENDIX

PUNCTUATION MARKS AND SYMBOLS

.	Full stop or period
,	comma
?	question mark
!	exclamation maek
-	hyphen
—	dash
"	open inverted commas / quotations
"	close inverted commas / quotations
( ) [ ] { }	brackets / parenthesis
A, B, C	Capital letters

a, b, c	small letters
a, b, c	cursives / italics
A, B, C	bold letters
=	equals
@	at
%	per cent
$	dollar
&	and
*	astric
'	apostrophe
__	underscore
#	harsh
/	oblique
\	backlash
:	colon
;	semi colon

< >	guillemets
Etc.	et cetra (and so on)
Eg.	example
i.e.	that is

REFERENCES

1. Encyclopedia Wikipedia

2. Encyclopedia Britannica

3. The Grammar Book - Marianne Celce - Murcia & Diane Larsen - Freeman Heinle & Heinle Publishers USA 1999

4. High School English Grammar - Wren and Martin - K & J Cooper Educational Publishers Bombay 1967

5. The New First Aid in English - Angus Maciver - Robert Gibson & Sons Glasgow.

6. Fundamentals of English Grammar - Betty S. Azar - Prentice Halls USA 1941

7. A modern En glish Course for Schools - A.M. Walinsley - United Tutorial Press - London. 1957

8. Notes from UPM English Units, UKM English Notes and UNITAR English Notes.

9. Common Errors in English - Richard Hughes & Carmel Heah - Fajar Bakti 1993

10. English Grammar and Analysis - W.Davidson and J.C.Alcock - Allman and Son London 1954

ANSWERS 1   NOUNS

1. boy - common noun
    hours - common noun

2. Kuala Lumpur - Proper noun
    city - common noun
    Malaysia - Proper noun

3. sea - common noun
    shoal of herring - collective noun

4. Honesty - Abstract noun
    policy - common noun

5. afternoon - common noun
    game of soccer - collective noun

6. members of staff - collective noun
    meeting - common noun

7. sultan - proper noun
    subjects - collective noun

8. hammer - common noun
    table - common noun

9. John Smith - proper noun
    school - collective noun
    morning - common noun

10. Professor - proper noun
    honour - abstract noun
    profession - common noum

ANSWERS 2   VERBS AND TENSES

Regular Verbs

Verbs	Past Tense	Past Participle
share	shared	shared
scare	scared	scared
dare	dared	dared
enjoy	enjoyed	enjoyed
surprise	surprised	surprised
play	played	played
want	wanted	wanted
shout	shouted	shouted
kill	killed	killed
fill	filled	filled

Irregular Verbs

eat	ate	eaten
write	wrote	written
arise	arose	arisen
awake	awoke	awakened
draw	drew	drawn
swim	swam	swum
see	saw	seen
drink	drank	drunk
break	broke	broken
bite	bit	bitten

Exercise 1

1. cry	6. skate
2. sings	7. collect
3. searches	8. plays
4. drives	9. flows
5. swim	10. get

2. In the Present continuous tenses:

1. The babies <u>were crying</u> because they were hungry.
2. The parrot <u>was singing</u> a lovely song.
3. Jayasinth <u>was searching</u> for her book.
4. The naughty boys <u>were shooting</u> the birds.
5. Rahman <u>was driving</u> his car carefully.
6. The boys <u>were skating</u> by the roadside.
7. The workers <u>were collecting</u> the fruit from the trees.
8. She <u>was playing</u> netball for her school.
9. The clear water <u>was flowing</u> along the hills.
10. They <u>were getting</u> water from the wells.

3. In the present perfect tenses:

1. The babies <u>have cried</u> because they were hungry.
2. The parrot <u>has sung</u> a lovely song.
3. Jayasinth <u>has searched</u> for her book.
4. The naughty boys <u>have shot</u> the birds.
5. Rahman <u>has driven</u> his car carefully.
6. The boys <u>have skated</u> by the roadside.
7. The workers <u>have collected</u> the fruit from the trees.
8. She <u>has played</u> netball for her school.
9. The clear water <u>has flown</u> along the hills.
10. They <u>have got</u> water from the wells.

4. In the Future Tenses:

1. The babies <u>will cry</u> when they are hungry.
2. The parrot <u>will sing</u> a lovely song.
3. Jayasinth <u>will search</u> for her book.
4. The naughty boys <u>will shoot</u> the birds.
5. Rahman <u>will drive</u> his car carefully.
6. The boys <u>will skate</u> by the roadside.
7. The workers <u>will collect</u> the fruit from the trees
8. She <u>will play</u> netball for her school.
9. The clear water <u>will flow</u> along the hills.
10. They <u>will get</u> their water from the wells

ANSWERS 3   ADJECTIVES

Exercise 1

1. few
2. heavy
3. several
4. every / its
5. live / dead

6. that / industrious
7. which
8. red
9. that/French/sports/excellent
10. comfortable

Exercise 2

Several answers are possible here.

1. first / clever (tall)
2. serious / simple
3. old
4. blatant / obvious
5. poor / handicapped

6. early
7. healthy
8. heavy / light
9. silent
10. great.

Exercise 3

1. tall / blue
2. beautiful / long
3. wet / cloudy
4. ugly / old /, hoarse, cracked.
5. lost / garden

6. new / great
7. new / silk
8. hill / short
9. newly / established / many / new
10. serious.

ANSWERS 4 PRONOUNS

Exercise 1

1. which
2. whose
3. that
4. that
5. that
6. that
7. that
8. whose
9. who
10. whose

Exercise 2

1. he, whom
2. He, I
3. her, I
4. He
5. me
6. me
7. they
8. him, her
9. I
10. who

Exercise 3

1. who
2. who
3. which
4. which
5. what
6. which
7. that
8. whom
9. which
10. who

ANSWERS 5   PREPOSITIONS

Exercise 1

1.	in	6.	under
2.	from	7.	down
3.	as	8.	from
4.	for	9.	to
5.	since	10.	from.

Exercise 2

1.	with	6.	for
2.	for	7.	about
3.	of	8.	to
4.	at, of	9.	to. about
5.	for	10.	from.

ANSWERS 6   ADVERBS

Exercise 1

1. once, twice - adverbs of number
2. very - adverb of degree
3. very - adverb of degree
4. away - adnerb of place
5. today - adverb of time
6. very - adverb of degree
7. ago - adverb of time
8. enough - adverb of degree
9. too - adverb of degree
10. tomorrow - adverb of time

Exercise 2

1. quite - adverb of degree
2. once - adverb of number
3. where - adverb of interrogation
4. too - degree
5. never - adverb of negation
6. now - adverb of time
7. very - adverb of degree
8. enough - adverb of degree
9. too - adverb of degree
10. somewhere - adverb of place

ANSWERS 7   CONJUNCTIONS

Exercise 1

1.	unless	-	subordinate conjunction
2.	if	-	subordinate conjunction
3.	unless	-	subordinate conjunction
4.	for	-	co-ordinating conjunction
5.	so	-	co-ordinating conjunction
6.	Either, or	-	correlative conjunction
7.	unless	-	subordinating conjunction
8.	till	-	subordinate conjunction
9.	lest	-	subordinate (condition)
10.	for	-	co-ordinating conjunction

Exercise 2

1. but		6. and	
2. but		7. but	
3. and		8. and	
4. and		9. but	
5. but		10. but.	

ANSWERS 9   ARTICLES

Exercise 1

1. a
2. An
3. A
4. a
5. an
6. an
7. the
8. A, the
9. the
10. an

Exercise 2

1. The sun rises in <u>the</u> east.
2. The brave soldier lost <u>an</u> arm in <u>the</u> battle.
3. The river was spanned by <u>an</u> iron bridge.
4. He likes to picture himself as <u>an</u> original thinker.
5. I have not seen him since he was <u>a</u> child.
6. The children suffered from Malaria.
7. The trip to Japan was arranged <u>a</u> week ago.
8. Livingstone was <u>a</u> great explorer.
9. We started late in <u>the</u> afternoon.
10. My favorite flower is <u>the</u> rose.

ANSWERS 10   GERUNDS AND INFINITIVES

Exercise 1

1. Hearing   -   Subject of the verb
2. Walking   -   Subject of the verb
3. spending   -   object of the verb
4. playing   -   object of the verb
5. Praising   -   subject. praising - object
6. Sining   -   subject of the verb
7. Standing   -   subject of the verb
8. Jumping   -   subject of the verb
9. winning   -   object of the verb
10. Reading   -   subject of the verb

Exercise 2

1. to   6. to
2. to   7. to
3. to   8. to
4. to   9. to
5. to   10. to

ANSWERS 11   SENTENCES TYPES AND ANALYSIS

Exercise 1

1. Statement	6. Exclamation
2. Question	7. Statement
3. Exclamation	8. Statement
4. Request	9. Exclamation
5. Question	10. Statement

Exercise 2

1. with a kind heart	-	adjective phrase
2. in a rude manner	-	adverbial phrase
3. such a thing	-	noun phrase
4. a house built of stone	-	adjective phrase
5. at this very moment	-	adverbial phrase
6. the silly question	-	noun phrase
7. with no writing in it	-	adjective phrase
8. on this very spot	-	adverbial phrase
9. in dark stables	-	adverbial phrase
10. without a friend	-	adjective phrase

Exercise 3

1. as one might expect him to do	-	adverbial clause
2. asked him many questions	-	noun clause
3. that had stopped	-	noun clause
4. where living was cheapest	-	adjective clause
5. saw the mirror broken	-	noun clause
6. how far it was	-	adverbial clause
7. because the night was dark	-	adverbial clause
8. have made a mistake	-	noun clause

9. after the work is finished   - adverbial clause

10. will miss the train   - noun clause

Exercise 4

1. The book which is red belongs to Ramlah.
   Or
   The red book belongs to Ramlah.
2. The woman who was selling flowers stood at the corner of the street.
3. The girl who fell heavily hurt herself.
4. The teacher praised the girls who had worked hard.
5. I visited the little cottage where I was born.
6. I was gazing out of the window when I saw a crowd.
7. Stephen was riding a horse which looked tired.
8. The old man went to the doctor who stayed next door.
9. The horse which was pulling a heavy load fell.
10. The man who caught a fish took iy home.

Exercise 5

1. Please tell me the wind direction.
2. They heard the news of his safety.
3. We saw them at six o'clock.
4. I admit my mistake.
5. She is an intelligent lady.
6. I cannot tell you her age.
7. They all believed the traveller's tale.
8. Jason lives in a very big house.
9. They asked me for my address.
10. Roshan lost his ticket because of his carelessness.
    or
    Careless Roshen lost his ticket.

ANSWERS 12   DIRECT AND INDIRECT SPEECH

Exercise 1

1. The teacher told the boys to sit down.
2. He told the servants to hurry up and not uaste aby nore time.
3. The Captain ordered his men to halt.
4. He told his friends that that is his new house,
5. She wrote that she was waiting for her son's return.
6. His father asked him if he was going home with him.
7. The man asked which way the puppy went.
8. He angrily remarked that he was a stupid fellow.
9. Anuar said that it was a nuisance.
10. I asked him if he knew the way home.

Exercise 2

1. He asked, "Did the dog die yesterday?"
2. He said, "I am getting tired now".
3. "Get out of my sight, Rahim", Anuar ordered.
4. "Let me go," she shouted.
5. "I am very clever," claimed Zahara.
6. "I want to be a doctor," said Rajan.
7. "We are all sinners," he said.
8. "Good deeds wash away sins," she remarked.
9. "Which is the proper way to answer the question?" the boy adked.
10. "What do you want?" he asked her.

ANSWER 13   ACTIVE AND PASSIVE VOICE

Exercise 1

1. The thief was caught by the police.
2. The boy was bitten by the dog.
3. The mouse was killed by the rat.
4. The horses were frightened by the sudden noise.
5. A letter will be written by his father.
6. A remarkable discovery was made by him.
7. That picture was drawn by my cousin.
8. The harvest was gathered by the farmer.
9. The trees were cut down by the men.
10. America was discovered by Christopher in 1492.

Exercise 2

1. Ahmad did not speak any word.
2. The teacher praised her.
3. The girl's work pleased the teacher.
4. The fire destroyed the town.
5. Her friend took her to the hospital.
6. The students lined the streets.
7. The wind blew down the trees.
8. A car knocked down the children.
9. The people welcomed the Sultan.
10. Khalil Gibran wrote *'Cry of the Graves'*.